DO YOU BELIEVE?
BIGFOOT

by Natalie Deniston

pogo

Ideas for Parents and Teachers

Pogo Books let children practice reading informational text while introducing them to nonfiction features such as headings, labels, sidebars, maps, and diagrams, as well as a table of contents, glossary, and index.

Carefully leveled text with a strong photo match offers early fluent readers the support they need to succeed.

Before Reading

- "Walk" through the book and point out the various nonfiction features. Ask the student what purpose each feature serves.
- Look at the glossary together. Read and discuss the words.

Read the Book

- Have the child read the book independently.
- Invite him or her to list questions that arise from reading.

After Reading

- Discuss the child's questions. Talk about how he or she might find answers to those questions.
- Prompt the child to think more. Ask: Do you believe in Bigfoot? Why or why not?

Pogo Books are published by Jump!
5357 Penn Avenue South
Minneapolis, MN 55419
www.jumplibrary.com

Copyright © 2025 Jump!
International copyright reserved in all countries. No part of this book may be reproduced in any form without written permission from the publisher.

Library of Congress Cataloging-in-Publication Data

Names: Deniston, Natalie, author.
Title: Bigfoot / by Natalie Deniston.
Description: Minneapolis, MN: Jump!, Inc., [2025]
Series: Do you believe? | Includes index.
Audience: Ages 7-10
Identifiers: LCCN 2023057290 (print)
LCCN 2023057291 (ebook)
ISBN 9798892132244 (hardcover)
ISBN 9798892132251 (paperback)
ISBN 9798892132268 (ebook)
Subjects: LCSH: Sasquatch—Juvenile literature.
Classification: LCC QL89.2.S2 D465 2025 (print)
LCC QL89.2.S2 (ebook)
DDC 001.944—dc23/eng/20231220
LC record available at https://lccn.loc.gov/2023057290
LC ebook record available at https://lccn.loc.gov/2023057291

Editor: Jenna Gleisner
Designer: Emma Almgren-Bersie

Photo Credits: Vac1/Shutterstock, cover (Bigfoot); awel Gaul/iStock, cover (background); Shutterstock, 1; JLFCapture/iStock, 3; Raggedstone/Shutterstock, 4; z1b/YayImages/SuperStock, 5; Bob Pool/Shutterstock, 6-7; AnnaStills/Shutterstock, 8; Norval Morrisseau, Windigo, ca. 1964, Tempera on Heavy Light Brown Building Paper. Collection of Glenbow, 9 (foreground); Olga Kovalenko/Shutterstock, 9 (background); EB Adventure Photography/Shutterstock, 10-11; John Zada/Alamy, 12-13; Roger Patterson and Robert Gimlin/Wikimedia, 14-15; Dyanna Yarbro/Dreamstime, 16; The Natural History Museum/Alamy, 17; Zuzha/Shutterstock, 18; INTERTOURIST/Shutterstock, 18-19; Roger Thornby/iStock, 20-21; katsuba_art/Shutterstock, 23.

Printed in the United States of America at Corporate Graphics in North Mankato, Minnesota.

TABLE OF CONTENTS

CHAPTER 1
Forest Creature 4

CHAPTER 2
Bigfoot Legends 8

CHAPTER 3
Bigfoot Theories 16

QUICK FACTS & TOOLS
Timeline 22
Glossary 23
Index 24
To Learn More 24

CHAPTER 1
FOREST CREATURE

A shadowy figure moves through the forest. It walks upright. It is covered in long hair. What is it? A bear? Maybe it is Bigfoot!

Bigfoot is said to be a creature that lives in forests. Some think it is **a primate** more than seven feet (2.1 meters) tall. Stories say its feet are nearly two feet (0.6 m) long!

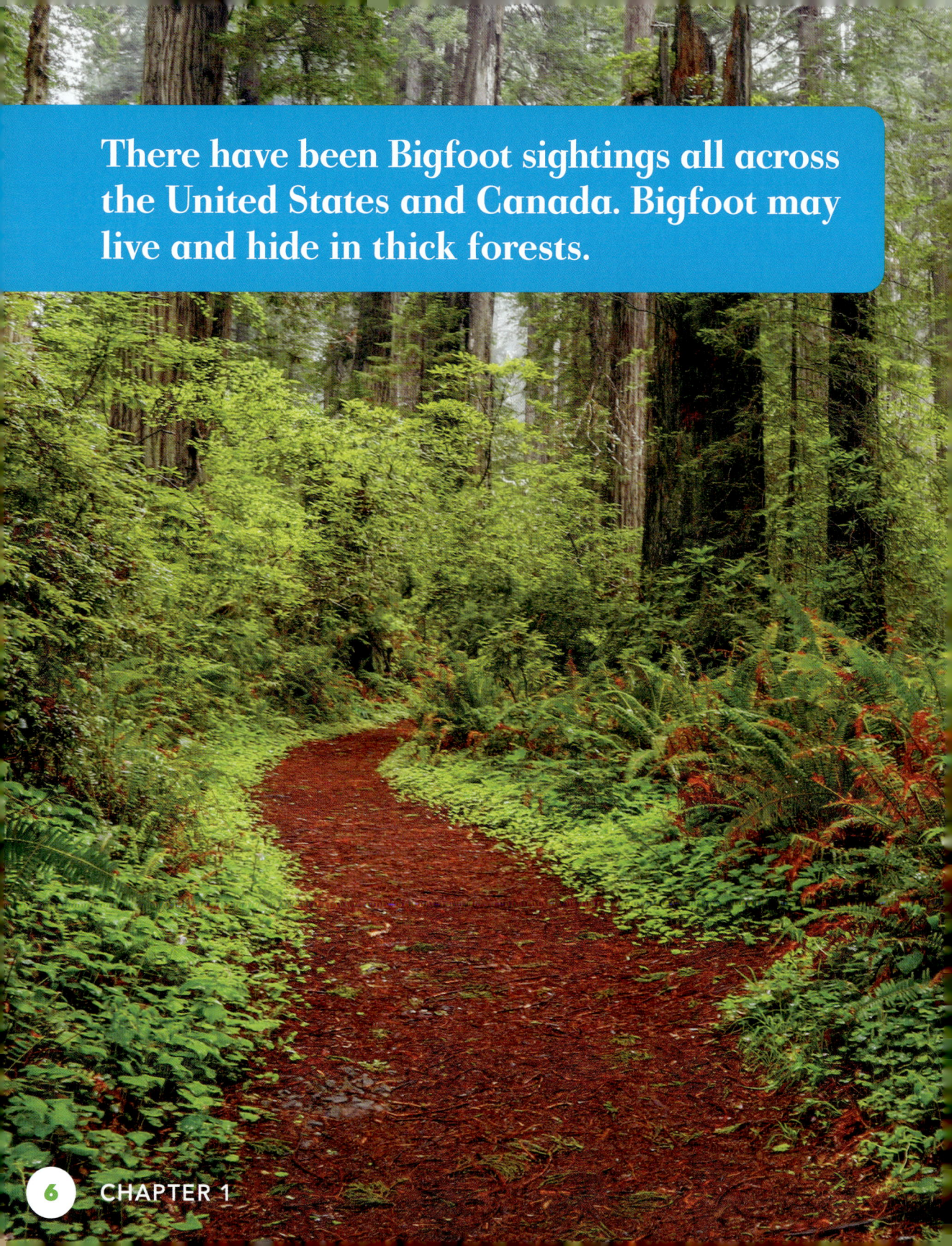

There have been Bigfoot sightings all across the United States and Canada. Bigfoot may live and hide in thick forests.

CHAPTER 1

TAKE A LOOK!

Which U.S. states have had the most Bigfoot sightings? Take a look!

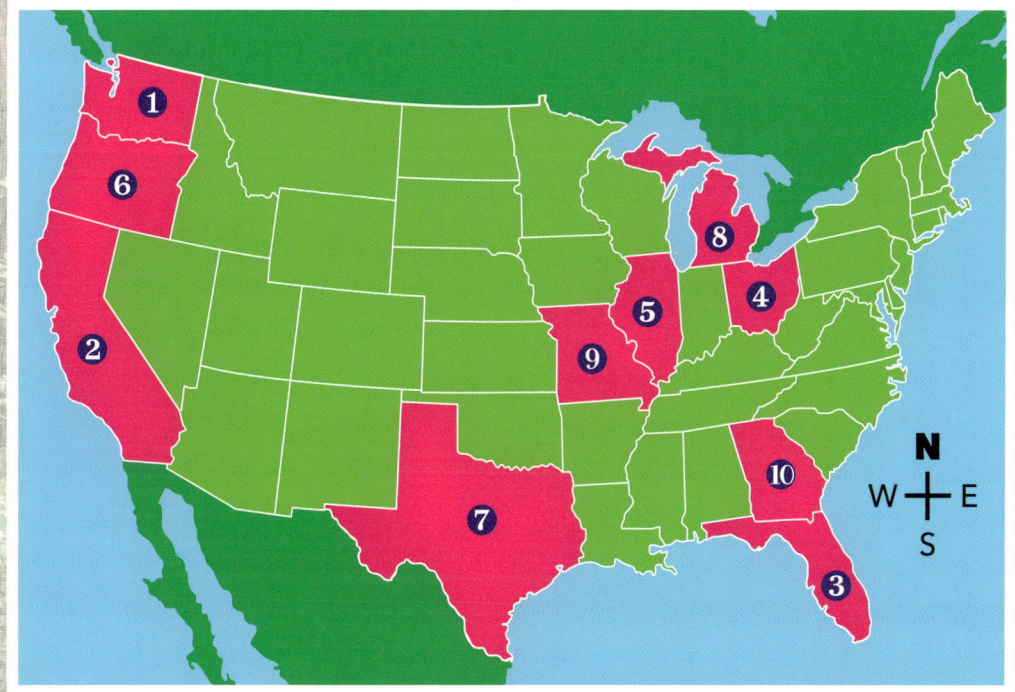

1. Washington
2. California
3. Florida
4. Ohio
5. Illinois
6. Oregon
7. Texas
8. Michigan
9. Missouri
10. Georgia

CHAPTER 2
BIGFOOT LEGENDS

Legends of Bigfoot have existed for hundreds of years. People still tell stories. Where do the stories come from?

wendigo

Some Native American **cultures** tell stories of similar creatures. The Algonquian peoples tell stories of wendigos. These are tall. They can be hairy. They live in the woods. Wendigos are said to attack people. They turn people into monsters.

In January 1811, David Thompson was **exploring**. He was in what is now Alberta, Canada. He wrote about his travels. He said he found **tracks** in the snow. They were 14 inches (36 centimeters) long. Some believe they were Bigfoot tracks!

DID YOU KNOW?

Bigfoot is also known as Sasquatch. This word comes from the Salish peoples of North America. It means "wild man."

CHAPTER 2

cast

In 1958, a man named Ray Wallace said he found giant tracks. They were near Bluff Creek, California. He made **casts** of them. Other people have since found tracks that might be from Bigfoot. They also make casts.

WHAT DO YOU THINK?

After Wallace died, his children said the tracks were a **prank**. Wallace used a wooden foot to make them. Why might someone pull pranks?

CHAPTER 2　13

In 1967, two men went to Bluff Creek. They looked for Bigfoot. They took a video of a creature walking. Many people believe the video shows Bigfoot.

WHAT DO YOU THINK?

Some people think the video is fake. They believe it is someone in a costume. Do you think it is real? Why or why not?

CHAPTER 2

CHAPTER 3
BIGFOOT THEORIES

Is Bigfoot wandering in the woods? Maybe. There are many **theories** about what Bigfoot could be.

Humans **evolved** from apes millions of years ago. Some people think humans may have evolved from a creature like Bigfoot. Bigfoot is sometimes called a "missing link" between humans and apes.

early humans

CHAPTER 3

Some people don't believe in Bigfoot at all! Bears live in many forests. They sometimes stand or walk on their back legs. From far away, bears might look like Bigfoot.

bear paw

CHAPTER 3

People disagree if Bigfoot is real or not. Some people say tracks or hair found in the forest are **evidence**. Others say these come from forest animals.

Many people like to look for Bigfoot. There are groups that search. Do you believe in Bigfoot? Would you like to find one?

DID YOU KNOW?

Stories similar to Bigfoot are shared around the world. Yeti may be a large, hairy creature in the Himalayas.

QUICK FACTS & TOOLS

TIMELINE

Stories of Bigfoot date back hundreds of years. Take a look!

1636
The first written account of wendigos is documented in what is now Quebec, Canada.

JANUARY 1811
David Thompson writes about large tracks found in what is now Alberta, Canada.

AUGUST 5, 1958
Ray Wallace makes fake Bigfoot tracks near Bluff Creek, California.

OCTOBER 20, 1967
Bob Gimlin and Roger Patterson film what they claim is Bigfoot near Bluff Creek.

1995
The Bigfoot Field Researchers Organization is founded. This group investigates reports of Bigfoot.

2024
No one has proven Bigfoot exists. Many people continue searching for evidence.

GLOSSARY

casts: Objects made by pouring liquid, such as plaster, into molds and letting them harden.

cultures: The ideas, customs, traditions, and ways of life of groups of people.

evidence: Information that proves if something is true.

evolved: Gradually changed from one generation to the next.

exploring: Traveling to discover new places or information.

legends: Stories passed down from earlier times that may be based on fact but are not entirely true.

prank: A joke or trick played on a person.

primate: A member of the group of mammals that includes apes, monkeys, and humans.

theories: Ideas or opinions that are based on some facts or evidence but are not proven.

tracks: Marks left behind by a moving animal or person.

INDEX

Algonquian peoples 9
apes 17
bear 4, 18
Bluff Creek, California 13, 14
Canada 6, 10
casts 13
costume 14
evidence 21
feet 5
forest 4, 5, 6, 18, 21
hair 4, 9, 21
legends 8
prank 13
primate 5
Salish peoples 10
Sasquatch 10
theories 16
Thompson, David 10
tracks 10, 13, 21
United States 6, 7
video 14
Wallace, Ray 13
wendigos 9
Yeti 21

TO LEARN MORE

Finding more information is as easy as 1, 2, 3.

1. Go to www.factsurfer.com
2. Enter "Bigfoot" into the search box.
3. Choose your book to see a list of websites.